PULL OVER

I spoke with my wife about writing this book, but I was a little indecisive about the title. I was sitting on the deck outside of our home contemplating it when my wife came out (while pantomiming holding a walkie talkie in her hand) and said, "what do the police say when they are behind you over the loudspeaker" to which I replied, "Pull Over" That is how this book got its name.

PULL OVER

Dedication

This book is dedicated to the men and women in law enforcement, STAY SAFE!

Table of contents

Introduction............................... 8
Before you start driving.....................14
As you are driving...........................16
During the traffic stop......................22
After the traffic stop........................30
Summary...32
References/resources........................35

Foreword

In my 27 years in Law Enforcement, I have discovered that it poses multiple challenges in our American society. The men and women who embark upon protecting and serving while enforcing the law, while working to maintain and not betray the public trust is what all police officers should strive for.

The author of this book is a staunch professional who has over 25 years of law enforcement and police training experience who I have had the pleasure of knowing for over five years. Having trained together, I have observed and been able to absorb his subject matter expertise on a plethora of law enforcement related topics gathered through his many years of work in this career field.

One of those areas is interpersonal communication skills and dealing with traffic stops. The use of courteous dialogue while enforcing traffic laws is meant to produce a positive interaction with the violator. With traffic stops being a dangerous scenario due to location, limited visibility and status of the offender, all officers are aware and keen on tactics to employ to keep themselves safe in the course of their duty. What an officer hopes to gain is public cooperation in which they follow instructions provided, maintain a calm demeanor, present all requested documents, and accept the decision of enforcement. Arguing the matter on the scene of the stop further escalates matters, know that the court is the medium to dispute their citation.

Robert S. Baker, Chief

Directorate of Emergency Services

ISBN: 9798534033823

Introduction

This book is intended as a guide to provide drivers with information that will help them to avoid a traffic stop by police, and how to handle the situation if it occurs. There is no magic formula, for the most part you as the driver of the motor vehicle determine if you get pulled over or not. The best way to avoid being pulled over is simple, operate your vehicle within the traffic regulations.

SOBERING STATISTICS

EVERY YEAR APPROXIMATELY 1.3 MILLION PEOPLE DIE IN CAR ACCIDENTS - AN AVERAGE OF 3,287 DEATHS PER DAY. *

- **GLOBALLY, CAR ACCIDENTS ARE THE LEADING CAUSE OF DEATH AMONG AGES 15-29 AND THE 9TH LEADING CAUSE OF DEATH FOR ALL PEOPLE. ***

- **IN 2019, 38,800 PEOPLE WERE KILLED IN CAR ACCIDENTS IN THE UNITED STATES. ***

- **STATISTICALLY TRAFFIC STOPS ARE ONE OF THE LEADING CAUSES OF DEATH/INJURY FOR POLICE OFFICERS. ***

BEFORE YOU START DRIVING

- ENSURE THAT YOU HAVE A VALID INSPECTION.

- WORKING TURN SIGNALS & BRAKE LIGHTS.

- PLEASE HAVE YOUR DRIVERS LICENSE, REGISTRATION, AND AN UPDATED INSURANCE CARD, ALSO KNOW WHERE THESE ITEMS ARE LOCATED.

- MAKE SURE TO USE A SEATBELT, IF THERE ARE PASSENGERS MAKE SURE THEY ARE WEARING THEIR SEATBELTS ALSO.

- **DON'T DRINK AND DRIVE.**

OBEY THE SPEED LIMIT

- EXCESSIVE SPEED IS A MAJOR CONTRIBUTOR TO ACCIDENTS.
- OBEY THE POSTED SPEED LIMIT.
- TRY TO FLOW WITH THE TRAFFIC.
- UNDERSTAND THAT YOU CAN BE ISSUED A TICKET IF YOU ARE GOING IN EXCESS OF 1 MILE PER HOUR ABOVE THE POSTED LIMIT.
- WHAT IF I AM FOLLOWING OR GOING WITH THE FLOW OF TRAFFIC? – YOU MAY ARGUE THAT IN COURT, **DO NOT ARGUE IT DURING THE TRAFFIC STOP.**

USE YOUR TURN SIGNALS

- THIS IS AN EASY ONE, WHENEVER YOU ARE GOING TO TURN OR MOVE TO ANOTHER LANE, USE THE TURN SIGNAL.

- EVERYONE FORGETS ON OCCASION, JUST DON'T MAKE A HABIT OF DOING SO.

- REMEMBER THE TURN SIGNAL ONLY LETS OTHER DRIVERS KNOW YOUR INTENTION. IT DOES NOT GIVE YOU THE RIGHT TO MOVE INTO ANOTHER LANE OR TURN IF IT ISNT SAFE TO DO SO.

- PLEASE REMEMBER TO TURN YOUR SIGNAL OFF, YOU DON'T WANT TO BE THAT PERSON THAT DRIVES FOR MILES WITH IT STILL BLINKING.

USE YOUR HEADLIGHTS, AND SLOW DOWN DURING INCLEMENT WEATHER

- AN ESTIMATED 22 PERCENT OF CRASHES ARE DUE TO INCLEMENT WEATHER.

- MOST STATES HAVE LAWS THAT APPLY TO DRIVING IN INCLEMENT WEATHER THAT SOME DRIVERS ARE UNAWARE OF.

- NORMALLY THEY REDUCE THE POSTED SPEED LIMIT BY 5-10 MPH.

- MANDATORY USE OF HEADLIGHTS DURING INCLEMENT WEATHER, NOT AN ISSUE WITH MOST VEHICLES THAT HAVE AUTOMATIC LIGHTS.

IF AN OFFICER PULLS BEHIND YOU IN TRAFFIC

- RELAX!
- THEY ARE PROBABLY THINKING ABOUT WHAT THEY ARE GOING TO HAVE FOR LUNCH.
- JUST CONTINUE TO DRIVE NORMALLY, YOU WILL KNOW SHORTLY IF THE OFFICER IS INTERESTED IN YOU.

IF THE LIGHTS ON THAT CRUISER COME ON AND THEY ARE DIRECTED AT YOU

- DON'T SLAM ON THE BRAKES!
- YOU CAN PUT YOUR BLINKERS OR TURN SIGNAL ON TO SHOW THAT YOU UNDERSTAND YOU ARE BEING PULLED OVER.
- SLOW DOWN AND TRY TO MANEUVER TO THE RIGHT SIDE OF THE ROAD (DEPENDENT ON YOUR LOCATION).
- IF YOU ARE APPROCHING THE CREST OF A HILL DRIVE A LITTLE FURTHER, DO THE SAME IF YOU ARE JUST ROUNDING A TURN.
- ONCE YOU SPOT A SAFE/ SUITABLE LOCATION, STOP THE VEHICLE.

AFTER YOU COME TO A COMPLETE STOP

- PLACE YOUR CAR IN PARK.
- DO NOT MAKE ANY UNNECESSARY MOVEMENTS.
- ROLL DOWN YOUR WINDOW.
- TURN ON YOUR INTERIOR LIGHT.
- PLACE YOUR HANDS AT THE 10/2 POSITION ON THE STEERING WHEEL.
- BE READY TO GREET THE OFFICER.
- THESE ACTIONS WILL LET THE OFFICER KNOW THAT YOU WISH TO COOPERATE AND WILL HELP THE TRAFFIC STOP GO SMOOTH.
- **REMAIN IN THE VEHICLE!**

OFFICERS INITIAL APPROACH

- **PLEASE DON'T MAKE ANY SUDDEN MOVEMENTS.**
- BE PREPARED TO HAND OVER YOUR DRIVERS LICENDE, REGISTRATION, AND INSURANCE CARD.
- HAND THEM TO THE OFFICER OUTSIDE THE WINDOW WHEN THEY ASK FOR THEM NOT BEFORE.
- THE OFFICER HAS THE RIGHT TO ASK YOU TO EXIT THE VEHICLE, IF YOU ARE ASKED TO STEP OUT OF THE VEHICLE BE GUIDED BY THE OFFICERS INSTRUCTIONS.
- IF THEY TAKE YOUR INFORMATION AND RETURN TO THEIR VEHICLE AWAIT THE OFFICERS RETURN.
- **DO NOT EXIT THE VEHICLE UNLESS TOLD TO DO SO!**

UPON SECOND APPROACH

- HANDS STILL AT THE 10/2 POSITION.
- BE PREPARED TO RECEIVE YOUR ITEMS BACK, REACH OUT FOR THEM.
- YOU MAY RECEIVE A WARNING, IF SO CONSIDER YOURSELF LUCKY!
- IF YOU GET A TICKET, DON'T FIGHT THE TICKET DURING THE STOP, DO THAT IN COURT.
- YOU MAY HAVE TO SIGN THE TICKET, THAT IS NOT AN ADMISSION OF GUILT, JUST ACKNOWLEDGING THAT YOU RECEIVED THE TICKET.
- ONCE THE STOP IS CONCLUDED THE OFFICER MAY DIRECT YOU BACK INTO TRAFFIC OR ADVISE YOU TO PULL OUT WHEN YOU DETERMINE IT IS SAFE TO DO SO.

AFTER LEAVING THE AREA OF THE STOP

- ONCE YOU LEAVE THE AREA OF THE STOP YOU MAY WANT TO CONSIDER PULLING INTO THE NEXT AVAILABLE GAS STATION OR REST AREA/PARKING LOT. THIS WILL GIVE YOU A FEW MINUTES TO DECOMPRESS BECAUSE FOR MANY PEOPLE BEING PULLED OVER MAY BE A LITTLE UNSETTLING. TAKE TIME TO GATHER YOURSELF AND EVALUATE YOUR ACTIONS WHILE DRIVING THAT CAUSED YOU TO BE PULLED OVER. ONCE YOU CALM DOWN AND FEEL YOU ARE READY TO CONTINUE TO YOUR DESTINATION YOU CAN GET BACK ON THE ROAD.
- **DRIVE SAFELY PLEASE!**

SUMMARY

- HAVE DL/REG/INSU HANDY.
- DON'T DRINK AND DRIVE.
- OBEY THE SPEED LIMIT/USE SIGNALS.
- SLOW DOWN DURING BAD WEATHER.
- RELAX, COPS ARE NOT OUT TO GET YOU.
- PULL OVER WHEN SAFE TO DO SO.
- COMPLETE STOP/ HANDS AT 10/2.
- NO SUDDEN MOVEMENTS.
- FOLLOW OFFICERS DIRECTIONS

DRIVE LIKE YOUR LIFE DEPENDS ON IT!

If you have any questions or recommendations for this book, please feel free to let me know and I will try to include that in an update. You may send suggestions and critiques to pulloverbook@gmail.com

Thank you and drive safe!

REFERENCES

The National Highway Traffic Safety Administration

The Uniform Crime Reporting (UCR) Program

www.ingramcontent.com/pod-product-compliance
Lightning Source LLC
Chambersburg PA
CBHW070907220526
45466CB00005B/2161